Majella

The Mothers' Saint

Thomas E. Tobin, C.SS.R.

Liguori
ONE LIGUORI DRIVE
LIGUORI MO 63057-9999

Imprimi Potest:
Edmund T. Langton, C.SS.R.
Provincial, St. Louis Province
The Redemptorists

Imprimatur:
+ George J. Gottwald
Vicar General of St. Louis

ISBN 978-0-7648-0431-1
© Liguori Publications
Printed in the United States of America
09 10 11   26 25 24

Liguori Publications, a nonprofit corporation, is an
apostolate of the Redemptorists. To learn more about the
Redemptorists, visit Redemptorists.com.

To order, call 800-325-9521
www.liguori.org

St. Gerard Majella
The Mothers' Saint

Thomas E. Tobin, C.SS.R.

Why is St. Gerard Majella invoked by thousands as "The Mothers' Saint"? It appears strange that a man, and a religious lay brother at that, should be so acclaimed. It might seem that a married woman, who had been blessed with the privilege of motherhood, would be chosen by divine providence for this office. However, the fact is that the countless favors and prodigies obtained for mothers and their children through the intercession of St. Gerard seem to suggest the role selected for him. Although the Church has not officially proclaimed him the patron of mothers, it is hoped that one day she may do so. During his life he helped mothers in need; since his death, in 1755, there has been a continuous flow of extraordinary favors granted to mothers who prayed to him; today there are millions who look to him for help in obtaining the blessing of motherhood and in the difficulties attendant on motherhood.

EARLY YEARS

Gerard, the youngest of the five children of Dominic and Benedetta Golella Majella, was born on April 6, 1726, in the small town of Muro, which is a few miles distant from Naples in southern Italy. He was very sickly at birth and was immediately taken to the Cathedral church for Baptism.

Even his childhood was marked by special graces from God. When he was only five, he was accustomed to go to a small chapel near his home to pray. Often he would return home from these visits with a loaf of bread. When asked about this, he would say that "a most beautiful boy" had given it to him. One day his sister, Elizabeth, followed him to the chapel and watched him while he knelt in prayer before a statue of the Blessed Mother holding the Child Jesus. Then she saw an amazing thing. The Child Jesus left His Mother's arms and came down to play with the little boy. Then, He gave Gerard a loaf of bread and returned to His Mother's arms. This was something of a prelude to the miraculous event in which the Archangel Michael gave him his first Holy Communion.

THE WORKING MAN

When Gerard was 12, the sudden death of his father made it necessary for him to leave school and to begin to work. His mother apprenticed him to a tailor so that he could follow the trade of his father. His employer took a strange dislike to him and often showered him with blows and curses. Gerard accepted the persecution as being permitted by God for his spiritual good. Once he was seen to smile even while he was being beaten, and when asked about this, he said: "I was smiling because I saw the hand of God striking me."

After apprenticing as a tailor, Gerard served for a while as a house boy for the Bishop of Lacedonia, who was recuperating in Muro. Again he manifested the virtue of patience by silently bearing the irascible temper of this otherwise worthy man. During this time one of his early miracles took place. One day he accidentally dropped the key of the house in the well. With saintly simplicity he lowered a small statue of the Infant Jesus into the well. Onlookers were amazed when Gerard raised the statue and the lost key was held in its hand.

RELIGIOUS VOCATION

Such a youth would naturally turn toward the religious life. Three times, however, he was refused admittance into one religious order because of his frail health. He was still determined to become a lay brother, and the occasion of a mission conducted by the Redemptorist Fathers in Muro gave him new hope. He asked to be admitted as a candidate in their order, but again was refused because they felt that his health would not be equal to the rigors of monastery life. So persistent was the young man, however, that Father Paul Cafaro, the superior of the missionaries, advised his mother to lock him in his room on the night they were leaving Muro, lest he try to follow them. Gerard's mother did so, but the next morning when she unlocked the door she found an empty bed, an open window from which hung a sheet, and a note on the table that read: "I have gone to become a saint."

Gerard had caught up with the missionaries just as they were leaving town. After many entreaties and refusals, Father Cafaro finally gave in and sent him on to the rector of the Redemptorist house at Iliceto with this note of recommendation: "I am sending you a useless lay brother."

The "useless" lay brother went on to do the work of four men, according to the testimony of those who worked with him. In his six short years as a Redemptorist, Gerard advanced rapidly in sanctity. His prayer life was continual and his spirit of obedience was so perfect that several times he even appeared at distant places in response to the unspoken requests of his absent superior. Even his confreres came to honor him as a saint.

Much of his life as a brother was spent in traveling with and assisting the missionaries. They deemed him an invaluable companion, because he had such remarkable success in bringing sinners to the sacraments and in inducing many to repair their past bad confessions. People followed him everywhere, and already called him "il santo" — the saint.

THE GREAT TRIAL

True sanctity must always be tested by the cross, and it was in 1754 that Gerard had to undergo a great trial, one that may well have merited for him the special power to assist mothers and their children. One of his works of zeal was that of encouraging and assisting girls who wanted to enter the convent. Often he would even secure the necessary dowry for some poor girl who could not otherwise be admitted into a religious order.

Neria Caggiano was one of the girls thus assisted by Gerard. However, she found convent life distasteful and within three weeks had returned home. To explain her action, Neria began to circulate falsehoods about the lives of the nuns, and when the good people of Muro refused to believe such stories about a convent recommended by Gerard, she determined to save her reputation by destroying the good name of her benefactor. Accordingly, in a letter to St. Alphonsus, the superior of Gerard, she accused the latter of sins of impurity with the young daughter of a family at whose house Gerard often stayed on his missionary journeys.

GERARD'S CONDUCT

Gerard was called by St. Alphonsus to answer the accusation. Instead of defending himself, however, he remained silent, following the example of his divine Master. In the face of his silence, St. Alphonsus could do nothing but impose a severe penance on the young religious. Gerard was denied the privilege of receiving Holy Communion, and forbidden all contact with outsiders.

It was not easy for Gerard to give up his labors in behalf of souls, but this was a small penance compared with being deprived of Holy Communion. He felt this so keenly that he even asked to be freed from the privilege of serving Mass for fear that the vehemence of his desire to receive would make him seize the consecrated host from the very hands of the priest at the altar.

Some time later Neria fell dangerously ill and wrote a letter to St. Alphonsus confessing that her charges against Gerard had been sheer fabrication and calumny. The saint was filled with joy by the news of the innocence of his son. But Gerard, who had not been depressed in the time of his trial, was not unduly elated in the hour of his vindication. In both cases he felt that the will of God had been fulfilled, and that was sufficient for him.

THE MIRACLE WORKER

Of few saints have there been so many wonderful events recorded as of Gerard. The process of his beatification and canonization reveals that his miracles were of the widest variety and profusion.

He frequently fell into ecstasy while meditating on God or His holy will, and at such times his body was seen raised several feet above the ground. There are authentic records to prove that on more than one occasion he was granted the unusual miracle of being seen and spoken to in two places at the same time.

Most of his miracles were performed in the service of others. Such extraordinary happenings as the following begin to seem commonplace when one reads of his life. He restored life to a boy who had fallen from a high cliff; he blessed the scanty supply of wheat belonging to a poor family and it lasted until the next harvest; several times he multiplied the bread that he was distributing to the poor. One day he walked across the water to lead safely to the shore a boatload of fishermen threatened by the stormy waves. Many times Gerard told people of secret sins on their souls which they had been ashamed to confess, and brought them to penance and forgiveness.

His miraculous apostolate for mothers also began during his lifetime. Once, as he was leaving the home of his friends, the Pirofalo family, one of the daughters called after him that he had forgotten his handkerchief. In a moment of prophetic insight Gerard said: "Keep it. It will be useful to you some day." The handkerchief was treasured as a precious souvenir of Gerard. Years later the girl to whom he had given it was in danger of death in childbirth. She remembered the words of Gerard, and called for the handkerchief. Almost immediately the danger passed and she delivered a healthy child. On another occasion the prayers of Gerard were asked by a mother when both she and her unborn child were in danger. Both she and the child came through the ordeal safely.

HIS DEATH

Always frail in health, it was evident that Gerard was not to live long. In 1755, he was seized by violent hemorrhages and dysentery and his death was expected at any moment. However, he had yet to teach a great lesson on the power of obedience. His director commanded him to get well, if it were God's will, and immediately his illness seemed to disappear and he left his bed to rejoin the community. He knew, however, that this cure was only temporary and that he had only a little over a month to live.

Before long he did have to return to his bed, and he began to prepare himself for death. He was absolutely abandoned to the will of God and had this sign placed on his door: "The will of God is done here, as God wills it and as long as He wills it." Often he was heard to say this prayer: "My God, I wish to die in order to do Thy most holy will." A little before midnight on October 15, 1755, his innocent soul went back to God.

HIS GLORIFICATION

At the death of Gerard, the Brother sacristan, in his excitement, rang the bell as if for a feast, instead of tolling it for a death. Thousands came to view the body of "their saint" and to try to find a last souvenir of the one who had helped them so often. After his death miracles began to be reported from almost all parts of Italy, attributed to the intercession of Gerard. In 1893, Pope Leo XIII beatified him, and on December 11, 1904, Pope Pius X canonized him as a saint.

WONDER WORKER OF OUR DAY

Devotion to St. Gerard spread rapidly beyond Italy and throughout the world and he came to be called "the wonder worker of our day." Because he had so often helped sinners to make a good confession, he was adopted by many as the patron of a good confession. Others revere the young apprentice tailor and Redemptorist lay brother as the patron of workingmen. Because he had so much difficulty getting into a religious order and because he sent so many girls to the convent he is often called upon as the patron of vocations.

THE MOTHERS' SAINT

Above all, the mothers of Italy took Gerard to their hearts and made him their patron. At the process of his beatification one witness testified that he was known as "il santo dei felice parti" — the saint of happy childbirth. His fame in this regard spread so that in many countries of the world mothers would not think of entering into their confinement without having a medal of St. Gerard. This devotion has become very popular in North America, both in the United States and Canada. Thousands of mothers have experienced his power. Many hospitals dedicate their maternity wards to him and give medals and prayer leaflets of St. Gerard to their patients. Thousands of children have been named after St. Gerard by parents who are convinced that it was his intercession that helped them to have healthy children. Even girls are named after him, and it is interesting how variously "Gerard" is given a feminine form. Some of the more popular names are: Gerarda, Geralyn, Gerardine, Gerianne, and Gerardette.

NOT ONLY A HELPER

St. Gerard obtains great favors for mothers and their children, but that is not his only office. He also teaches parents and especially mothers the duties of their state in life. The terrible and all too common evils in marriage today are the sins of contraception and abortion. Under pretext of poor health, or lack of material means, or fear of the future or of what others may say, there are those who limit their families by methods considered sinful by the Church. The only adequate defense against this evil is an unlimited trust in God. God made marriage a sacrament and thereby promised to provide every Christian married couple with all the graces necessary to fulfill the laws He had made for marriage.

One of Gerard's greatest virtues was trust, and his favorite slogan was "God will provide." Once while he was on a pilgrimage with some clerical students, he used their last few coins to buy some flowers for the altar. When he placed the flowers before the altar he said: "Lord, I have taken care of You. Now you take care of my students and me." And the Lord did provide sufficient money for the rest of the trip. When the false accusation was made against him, to all the entreaties of friends to defend himself he replied: "It is for God to see to that." In poor health and in danger of death his trust in God did not waver one bit. Thus Gerard showed himself as a model that mothers can imitate in the confidence in God on which marriage must be based, if they are to avoid the forces of "anti-life."

PRAYERS

For Motherhood

Good St. Gerard, powerful intercessor before the throne of God, wonder-worker of our day, I call upon you and seek your aid. You know that our marriage has not as yet been blessed with a child and how much my husband and I desire this gift. Please present our fervent pleas to the Creator of life from whom all parenthood proceeds and beseech Him to bless us with a child whom we may raise as His child and heir of heaven. Amen.

For a Mother with Child

Almighty and everlasting God, through the power of the Holy Spirit, you prepared the body and soul of the Virgin Mary to be a worthy dwelling place of your divine Son. You sanctified St. John the Baptizer, while still in his mother's womb. Listen now to my prayer. Through the intercession of St. Gerard, watch over my child and me; protect us at the time of delivery. May my child receive the saving graces of Baptism, lead a Christian life, and, together with all the members of our family, attain everlasting happiness in heaven. Amen.

For a Sick Child

St. Gerard, who, like the Savior, loved children so tenderly and by your prayers freed many from disease and even death, listen to us who are pleading for our sick child. We thank God for the great gift of our son (daughter) and ask Him to restore our child to health if such be His holy will. This favor, we beg of you through your love for all children and mothers. Amen.

In Thanks for a Safe Delivery

Good St. Gerard, patron of mothers, assist me in thanking God for the great gift of motherhood. During the months of my waiting, I learned to call upon you and placed the safety of my child and myself under your powerful protection. The great lesson of your trust in God sustained me; your slogan, "God will provide," became my hope and consolation. I thank God for a healthy and normal baby and my own good health. Help me to prize the great treasure of motherhood and obtain for me the grace to raise my child as a child of God.

In gratitude, I will continue to call upon you and will tell other mothers about their special patron and friend. Amen.

For Special Blessings

Almighty and loving Father, I thank You for giving St. Gerard to us as a most appealing model and powerful friend. By his example, he showed us how to love and trust You. You have showered many blessings on those who call upon him. For Your greater glory and my welfare, please grant me the favors which I ask in his name.

(Here mention them privately)

And you, my powerful patron, intercede for me before the throne of God. Draw near to that throne and do not leave it until you have been heard. 0 good saint, to you I address my fervent prayers; graciously accept them and let me experience in some way the effects of your powerful intercession. Amen.

In Time of Trial

St. Gerard, whose heart went out to the unfortunate, who relieved so many poor, healed so many sick, comforted so many afflicted, I am worried and troubled as I kneel at your feet. In vain do I seek this world's help and consolation. Graciously pray for me, St. Gerard, that, being freed from this trial or strengthened to bear it for the love of God, I may praise and thank God and serve Him with greater love and fervor. Amen.

For a Good Confession

St. Gerard, patron of a good confession, who gave courage to souls whom fear and shame had overcome, who gave sorrow to their hearts, resolution to their wills, truth to their faltering lips, help me to make a good confession. Enable me to know my sins, to be truly sorry for them, and to be firmly resolved, with God's grace, never to sin again. Help me to confess my sins humbly and sincerely, to confess them to our Lord himself. Stand by me in this confession, gentle saint. Amen.

For Respect of Life

St. Gerard Majella, women the world over have adopted you as their patron in the joys and fears of childbearing. Today, we invoke your intercession for the pro-life movement. Pray that all will look upon human life as a gift from God, not as an unwanted burden to be destroyed. Assist the efforts of those on earth who are enlisted in the crusade of promoting the dignity and value of all human life, particularly the unborn. This we ask through Christ, our Lord. Amen.

LITANY OF ST. GERARD

(For Private Use Only)

Lord, have mercy on us

Christ, have mercy on us.

Lord, have mercy on us.

Christ, hear us.

Christ, graciously hear us.

God the Father of Heaven,
  HAVE MERCY ON US.

God the Son, Redeemer of the world,
  HAVE MERCY ON US.

God the Holy Spirit,
  HAVE MERCY ON US.

Holy Trinity, One God,
  HAVE MERCY ON US.

Holy Mary, Mother of Perpetual Help,
  PRAY FOR US.

St. Joseph, Foster-father of Christ,

St. Alphonsus, founder of the Congregation
  of the Most Holy Redeemer,

St. Gerard, endowed with extraordinary graces from early childhood,

St. Gerard, perfect type of a faithful servant,

St. Gerard, shining example for the laboring classes,

St. Gerard, great lover of prayer and work,

St. Gerard, seraphic adorer of the Most Blessed Sacrament,

St. Gerard, living image of the Crucified Savior,

St. Gerard, most devoted client of the Immaculate Virgin Mary,

St. Gerard, bright mirror of innocence and penance,

St. Gerard, admirable model of heroic obedience,

St. Gerard, silent victim of ignominious calumny,

St. Gerard, great before God by thy deep humility,

St. Gerard, truly wise by thy childlike simplicity,

St. Gerard, supernaturally enlightened in divine mysteries,

St. Gerard, solely desirous of pleasing God,

St. Gerard, zealous promoter of the conversion of sinners,

St. Gerard, wise counselor in the choice of vocation,

St. Gerard, enlightened guide in the direction of souls,

St. Gerard, kind friend of the poor and distressed,

St. Gerard, safe refuge in sickness and sorrow,

St. Gerard, wonderful protector of unbaptized children,

St. Gerard, compassionate intercessor in all our wants,

St. Gerard, exalted by God through astonishing miracles,

St. Gerard, ornament and glory of the Redemptorist Order,

Lamb of God, who takes away the sins of the world, SPARE US, O LORD.

Lamb of God, who takes away the sins of the world, GRACIOUSLY HEAR US, O LORD.

Lamb of God, who takes away the sins
of the world, HAVE MERCY ON US,
O LORD.

Pray for us, St. Gerard,

That we may be made worthy of the
promises of Christ.

Let Us Pray

O God, Who deigned to draw St. Gerard unto
Thyself from his youth; and to make him
conformable to the image of Thy Crucified
Son; grant, we beseech Thee, that following
his example, we may be transformed into the
same image, through the same Christ Our
Lord. Amen.